W9-BQV-799

J594 S/8   1/13

DATE DUE			
MAY 2 0 2013			
JUL 2 9 2013			
AUG 1 9 2013			
JUN 0 7 2016			

DEMCO 38-296

STRANGE Life Cycles

The Bizarre Life Cycle of an OCTOPUS

By Therese Shea

Gareth Stevens
Publishing

Please visit our website, www.garethstevens.com. For a free color catalog of all our high-quality books, call toll free 1-800-542-2595 or fax 1-877-542-2596.

Library of Congress Cataloging-in-Publication Data

Shea, Therese.
The bizarre life cycle of an octopus / Therese Shea.
    p. cm. — (Strange life cycles)
Includes index.
ISBN 978-1-4339-7056-6 (pbk.)
ISBN 978-1-4339-7057-3 (6-pack)
ISBN 978-1-4339-7055-9 (library binding)
1. Octopuses—Life cycles—Juvenile literature. I. Title.
QL430.3.O2S54 2013
594'.56—dc23

2011052424

First Edition

Published in 2013 by
Gareth Stevens Publishing
111 East 14th Street, Suite 349
New York, NY 10003

Copyright © 2013 Gareth Stevens Publishing

Designer: Andrea Davison-Bartolotta
Editor: Kristen Rajczak

Photo credits: Cover, pp. 1, 4, 13, 14, 17, 21 Shutterstock.com; pp. 5, 15, 19 iStockphoto.com; p. 7 Rodger Klein/WaterFrame/Getty Images; p. 9 Robert F. Sisson/National Geographic/Getty Images; p. 11 Rodger Klein/WaterFrame/Getty Images; p. 20 Jorgen Jessen/AFP/Getty Images.

Printed in the United States of America

CPSIA compliance information: Batch #CS12GS: For further information contact Gareth Stevens, New York, New York at 1-800-542-2595.

Contents

Words in the glossary appear in **bold** type the first time they are used in the text.

How Bizarre!

An octopus looks creepy! Its soft body, or mantle, and eight long arms can squeeze into tight spaces. The octopus can do this because it's an invertebrate, which means it doesn't have a backbone. In fact, it doesn't have bones at all!

Octopuses breathe with gills, just like fish. Water flows into the mantle through the gills and out through a tube called a siphon. But it's not just an octopus's body that's weird. The octopus has a pretty **bizarre** life cycle, too!

octopus arm

THE FACTS OF LIFE

Octopuses are part of an animal group called mollusks. A feature of most mollusks is their shell, but octopuses don't have one.

Octopuses belong to a group of mollusks called cephalopods. "Cephalopod" means "head-foot." An octopus's "feet" (or arms) are attached to its "head" (or mantle).

5

Time to Mate

An octopus's life begins in an egg after a male and female octopus **mate**. The male octopus has one arm that looks a bit different from the other seven. He uses this arm to give the female special cells to **fertilize** her eggs. She stores these cells in her body until she lays eggs.

At least one kind of octopus—the blanket octopus—has a bizarre mating habit. The male actually takes off his arm and gives it to the female! Male octopuses die soon after mating.

THE FACTS OF LIFE

Scientists think that the female octopus makes a special **chemical** in her body that draws a mate—and keeps him from eating her!

Some mother octopuses—such as this blue-ringed octopus—carry their eggs with them.

A Mother's Care

Mother octopuses may lay thousands of eggs. Each egg has a string attached that the mother ties to many other eggs. She hangs these strings of eggs from the roof of her den.

The mother octopus guards her eggs and blows water at them so they get **oxygen**. She keeps them clean using the **suckers** on her arms. She spends all her time with the eggs and doesn't eat. This causes the mother octopus to slowly weaken. When her eggs finally hatch, she dies.

THE FACTS OF LIFE

Giant Pacific octopuses can lay as many as 100,000 eggs!

This tiny octopus—about the size of a grain of rice—has just burst from its egg. Baby octopuses that haven't hatched yet can be seen inside two other eggs.

9

Young Octopuses

Newborn octopuses, called paralarvae, swim up and join the **plankton** drifting on the ocean's surface. They eat anything they can catch. After a few weeks, most baby octopuses swim down to the ocean floor.

Scientists don't know much about the lives of young octopuses. They do know that very few live to become adults. While baby octopuses float, they're in danger of being eaten by whales and many kinds of fish. When they've grown larger, **predators** include seals, sharks, eels, dolphins—and even other octopuses!

THE FACTS OF LIFE

Octopuses often make a den out of rocks on the ocean floor. An octopus's den is also called a garden.

This young octopus has made its home in a bottle!

Now You See It . . .

Did you know that some kinds of octopuses change color and shape to match their surroundings? They have special skin cells and **muscles** that work quickly to blend in with rocks and other things in the ocean.

When an octopus fears a predator's attack, it may release a dark inky liquid from its body. An ink cloud can hide the octopus and help it escape. Sometimes the ink looks like an octopus, drawing the predator away from the real octopus.

THE FACTS OF LIFE

There are more than 250 species, or kinds, of octopuses. However, scientists only know about a few of them.

This mimic octopus can make itself look like a giant crab!

A Bad Bite

Octopuses don't just run and hide from predators. They're predators, too. Octopuses have excellent eyesight and mostly hunt at night. They use their long arms to reach creatures in tight spaces. The suckers on an octopus can taste whatever they touch so the octopus knows if it has found food! It may use its ink cloud to hide before attacking an animal.

Octopuses have a sharp beak to bite their victims and break through shells. **Venom** in their spit breaks down the insides of an animal so it's easier to eat.

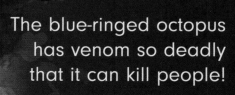

THE FACTS OF LIFE

The blue-ringed octopus has venom so deadly that it can kill people!

Octopuses like to eat crabs, lobster, clams, and shrimp. A giant Pacific octopus may eat birds and sharks, too!

Adult Octopuses, Big and Small

Most octopuses grow to be about 1.6 feet (50 cm) long. They usually weigh less than 22 pounds (10 kg). However, there are octopuses much smaller and much bigger. The smallest octopus is the California octopus, which is only about 1 inch (2.5 cm) long. The giant Pacific octopus can grow to be over 30 feet (9 m) long and weigh 100 pounds (45 kg).

All octopuses have long arms lined with suckers. Female giant Pacific octopuses have 280 suckers on each arm!

THE FACTS OF LIFE

Octopuses don't have tentacles. Tentacles are usually longer than arms and only have suckers at their tip. Squids, for example, have two tentacles along with their eight arms.

Giant Pacific octopuses are commonly reddish brown or pink.

Senescence

Once octopuses are fully grown, they look for a mate. That means the beginning of the end of the life cycle of the octopus.

The last stage of the cycle is called senescence (sih-NEH-suhns). It happens to males after mating and to females after laying their eggs. They stop eating, are unaware of predators, and don't care for themselves in other ways, too. Death soon follows. Many octopuses only live about a year, while the largest live for about 4 years.

THE FACTS OF LIFE

If a predator catches an octopus's arm, the octopus can leave its arm behind! The octopus can then grow another arm.

All the many kinds of octopus go through senescence.

So Smart!

Scientists have learned that octopuses are the smartest invertebrate animals. They have large brains for invertebrates, and their brains have areas for memory and learning. They like to play and take things apart. Giant Pacific octopuses have learned to open jars and even solve mazes! In fact, it's hard to keep an octopus in a tank because it'll figure out how to get out.

Scientists hope to keep learning more about octopuses in the future. You can learn more about them—and their bizarre lives— at your local aquarium!

An octopus at Denmark's Aquarium tries to open a jar to get to a crab inside.

The Life Cycle of an Octopus

male and female octopus mate

male octopus dies

female octopus lays eggs

eggs hatch

mother octopus dies

paralarvae swim to ocean's surface

most young octopuses return to the deep ocean and grow into adults

Glossary

bizarre: very strange or unusual

chemical: matter that can be mixed with other matter to cause changes

fertilize: to add male cells to a female's eggs to make babies

mate: to come together to make babies. Also, one of two animals that come together to make babies.

muscle: one of the parts of the body that allow movement

oxygen: a gas that is necessary for people and animals to breathe

plankton: a tiny plant or animal that floats in the ocean

predator: an animal that hunts other animals for food

sucker: part of an animal used for holding on to things

venom: poisonous matter created by an animal and passed on by a bite or sting

For More Information

Books

Gross, Miriam J. *The Octopus*. New York, NY: PowerKids Press, 2006.

Lunis, Natalie. *Blue-Ringed Octopus: Small but Deadly*. New York, NY: Bearport Publishing, 2010.

Spilsbury, Louise. *Octopus*. Chicago, IL: Heinemann Library, 2011.

Websites

Common Octopus
animals.nationalgeographic.com/animals/invertebrates/common-octopus/
Hear what an octopus sounds like, and read more about octopuses' lives in the deep sea.

Giant Pacific Octopus
nationalzoo.si.edu/Animals/Invertebrates/Facts/cephalopods/FactSheets/Pacificoctopus.cfm
Learn about the largest octopus in the world.

Index